D0585696

The Running
of the Salmon

TEN SILVER SALMON

THE RUNNING
OF THE SALMON

Eric Taverner &
W. Barrington Browne

LONDON
GEOFFREY BLES
1954

Printed in Great Britain by
Butler & Tanner Ltd Frome
for Geoffrey Bles Ltd
52 Doughty Street London W.C.1

First published in 1954

The Running of the Salmon

THE ZONES THROUGH WHICH SMOLTS PASS OUT-wards and salmon pass inwards are here linked with four sea-animals, but not precisely. The shallow waters of shore and estuary have been associated with the shore-skipper Gammarus, a near relative of the fresh-water shrimp. The second zone is that of the prawn Leander, a surprisingly good swimmer, as the name suggests. The copepod Calanus, beloved of herring, has been chosen to represent the next. The outermost bears the name of Euphausia, another free-swimming copepod, which ranges far, either passively or in still waters and weak currents rowing itself along with its little oars. Those names are, as it were, stages along the road that create the illusion of travel. No-one has discovered whither goes the feed-ing salmon, which may indeed be a comparatively rare fish in the sea.

But wherever it does go, there is Euphausia.

Where lies the land to which the ship would go?
Far, far ahead, is all her seamen know.
And where the land she travels from? Away,
Far, far behind, is all that they can say.

ARTHUR HUGH CLOUGH, 1819–1861

LEAVING EUPHAUSIA, WHICH IS SOMEWHERE TO the east of the Great Abyss and south of the frigid sea-mountains and valleys that descend from the Ultimate Isles, passing through the wide spaces of Calàn and Leander, they entered the shallow regions of Gammar. Ten silver salmon, all females together, all of them bound for the spawning-beds and without a thought for the males.

All of them came fully fed, but fasting, and with a common purpose. Why they did so and why they all left together—and we have no reason to suppose they could discuss these matters between themselves—are questions as yet beyond the wisdom of man.

The sojourn in the sea of feeding salmon varies much in its duration, from fourteen months, when they come in as early grilse, to five years. They may return to the river at any time of the year. Their choice of the time to return, if they have one, is incomprehensible to us. It may be that their behaviour is due to inheritance, or one imposed by a river upon its frequenters, or one proper to the fish itself. Upon reflection I think it better not to try and compute the degree of probability, but rather to admit that we know absolutely nothing about it.

At length the Ten arrived at the selvedge around the coast and turned westwards for a day and night. They went that way, toward the setting of the sun, not through any exercise of free will nor because they were so predestined, but in obedience to the dictate of the Great Mathematician, he who decides whether a penny shall come up heads or tails.

Not finding that taste in the water for which they were seeking, they hesitated and swam eastwards. A hunting porpoise came curveting through the sunlit, offshore waters.

> *Ten silver salmon*
> *Striking for a line.*
> *A herring-hog ate one of them*
> *And then there were nine.*

In the afternoon the Nine salmon passed the point where they had made their landfall and still went on. They followed their quest through the narrows between a rocky islet and the mainland; but . . .

Nine silver salmon
Streaking through the strait.
A seal chopped the last behind
And then there were eight.

At last, after many trials and essays, they discovered the first of the things for which they were being compelled by some strange force within them to seek. Not every salmon is so fortunate. Many must fail in the search and wander, accepting in the last resort a strange river, for there are no guides to show them the way. It has been said that returning fish are attracted by the taste of the water of their natal stream. That means their memory of it is still strong after three years at sea. But can that be true?

Over the bar against the racing tide went the Eight. They followed the brackish water up the sea-wracked lanes, a snaky course which led to a large draught, as fishermen call a pit, wherein, year after year, freshly arrived salmon are to be found lying. There at the next draw luck was with them. The long, grasping arm of a seine-net came round just inside them, as they lay along the outer edge of the pit.

Up with the ebb and down with the flood, they gradually worked their way toward the river. (That I know, for I saw them pass under the long bridge and, as I looked down on them, I noticed that one bore a large white patch on the head. Thereafter I followed them in imagination.) And all the time they spent in the estuary, their blood was being balanced in pressure for life in fresh water.

During the third night they dropped back to meet the salt flood and lay in the perilous draught above the bridge. But the turn of that tide brought a turn of luck.

Eight silver salmon
Freshly in from sea.
Netsmen took five of them
And then there were three.

There had been heavy rain in the hills and on high ground of the watershed. A spate was travelling down; and men upstream were watching anxiously the level of the river, as it crept up to and then covered the familiar marks on stone and buttress. When, at length, the swollen landwater entered the head of the estuary, the Call came; and the Three slipped upwards out of reach of the tide. Eagerly they embraced the current and pushed their way against it, for such is the nature of all Trouts and Salmons.

At last, they came to the foot of white water falling brokenly into a pool below a weir. Some lampreys were there, having recently arrived from sea. They were engaged in preparations for spawning

12

Barrington Browne

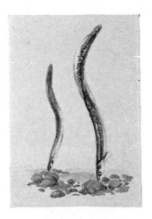

and were standing on their heads, as they lifted stones from the river-bed and, gripping them by suction, allowed themselves to be carried downstream, until they reached the place where a spawning-nest was being constructed. Quite different from the salmon's way.

At first light they jumped at the tumbling water, again and again, until they succeeded in gripping it with flanks and tail, and so passed over. An early run of small seatrout was there, too. To them the weir seemed to present little difficulty. They leapt with astounding agility from the turbulence, flung themselves high into the air and easily cleared the edge of the fall.

When salmon finally succeed at a difficult place, they do so by persistency and plough their way through the water. Usually they are not as expert at jumping as are young seatrout. There was a place on a West Highland river, where salmon might be seen swimming vertically up within the veil of falling water; but to do this there had to be volume enough to give a solid grip for the tail. They did this in preference to leaping and showed themselves only for an instant by a flick of the tail as they crossed over to the river above.

14

THE PERILOUS DRAUGHT

The next day, the fourth since leaving the estuary, the last of the female sea-lice slipped from them.

What a different world this was to prove for those Three! A narrow world. A shallow world. A bright light above. Things moving across a circular window overhead and, beyond that, moving about steeply descending slopes. Violent flashes, whenever the surface was broken or scratched by leaf, by insect or by catspaw of wind. Boulders to avoid below and weed-beds. Water ever varying in temperature, in colour, in clarity, in taste and in the force with which it pressed down against them. Some of these things could hardly mean to them what they mean to us and may mean nothing. But are not salmon the children of their own environments, the grey sea and the unsleeping river?

Maintenance of balance became the ever-present duty; and the need to keep head to stream had become vital. Unceasingly the current tried all roads to bear upon the flanks of the fish. Had it got a purchase upon the flanks of any one of them, it would have swept it seawards. As long as the life of a fish endures, there will continue this struggle, which until death supervenes it only just manages to win.

From one force at least, from the downward pull of gravity, it is

However, a salmon lying well below them, near the draw of the pool, found the fly more convincing; for, undoubtedly, some fish are more easily tempted than are others. Its reflex was awakened by some movements of the fly, which it promptly seized; and all the pool was thoroughly disturbed by its efforts to escape from the unaccustomed restraint which was holding it back from the up-stream search. At once the interest of the Three was reawakened. Curiosity? Rapacity? Who knows? So we call it conditioned reflex —and thus divert attention to the problem of defining that term precisely!

Again, the invisible force began driving them upstream, a force which was irresistible. Two days of rain over the watershed gave them good running-water. And the Three moved up, under the shadows of trees and under bridges thrown across the watery high-way, as though it were spanned by a series of triumphal arches. Why not? Those Three were showing themselves utterly constant in their determination to find an Unknown Place for an Unknown Purpose. Whether any one of them would finally succeed was still uncertain and depended upon the Law of Chance.

Not all salmon ascend to the head-waters of the river. Some come very late in summer from the sea and make their redds in the gravel of the middle and lower reaches. On occasions, autumn salmon have already assumed their spawning-dress, by the time they leave salt water, and may not go far above the reach of the tide to achieve their purpose. Whether this happens because time is against them, or whether these belated fish have, in fact, already ascended far enough to regain the areas where they were hatched, is an open question and one of great importance in the conservation of the stock.

It is certainly quite clear that eggs are not distributed by being scattered broadcast and carried by the current in the same way as

Triumphal Arches

eggs and larvae at sea. They are distributed throughout the river by the spacing-out of the breeding adults. It is, however, dangerous to suggest that this behaviour and the wide choice of spawning-site are so-called 'provisions of nature' to secure distribution.

The 'taking mood', which on most days in the height of the season comes over ascending salmon about the same hour up and down the river's length, had not passed them by. But no angler had come their way at those times; although many were the skilfully fished flies, minnows and other lures they had watched and often had followed. Few, except anglers, realize how subtle are the timing and manner of these things: the right size of fly rightly presented and the mood of the salmon to take it.

One day an angler with murder in his heart (I know he had, for I heard what he said) put over the pool where the Three were then lying a large pink prawn, bristling with hooks. The hour of one of them had come. What followed might have been the lot of any of the Three. She to whom the prawn came nearest, seized it instantly. Soon afterwards, for the trace was of wire, her companions saw her drawn irresistibly through a ragged rent in the surface.

N.º 1

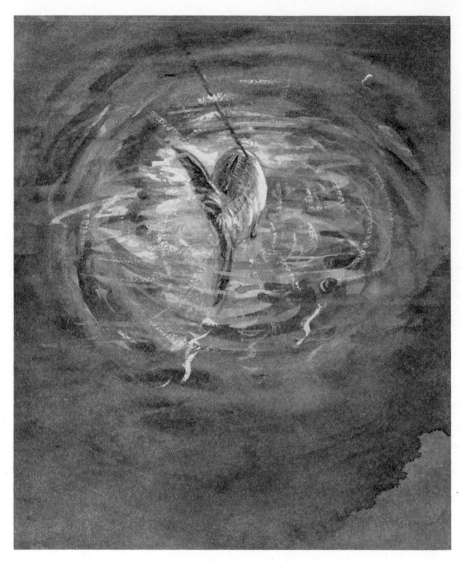

ARTIST'S NOTE: *A fish's view of the picture overleaf. It really should be drawn on the ceiling by Michelangelo!*

Three darkening salmon
Wondering what to do.
The smallest took the spinning prawn
And then there were two.

The water flowed on. The wound in it was healed. The surface became once more a moving mirror.

Does this return to the river awaken memories of a former fresh-water life? memories of insects above, on or under the surface of the water? Such ideas are voiced to explain why adult salmon, which never feed in fresh water as they ascend, rise to the feathered lures that by courtesy are called flies. Improbables both.

No salmon can fail to see trout in its vicinity taking nymphs and, also, insects caught in the surface-film. On rare occasions it will be observed doing the same. It has been seriously suggested that a salmon, so engaged, is actually feeding and is obtaining nourishment to offset the effect of abstinence in fresh water. As well offer comfits to an elephant!

All the summer through the Two waited—restlessly it seemed to me watching from the bank—for the next of a succession of steps

upwards, a mile or it might be two miles nearer The Place, the very place, maybe, where the Two had been hatched out. Who knows? To a salmon the end of their quest must always appear to lie just round the corner, for that, surely, is the limit of their geographical knowledge.

Thus, travelling at a pace suited to the season, they forged their way upwards in good running-water as far as opportunity allowed. They stopped when they could proceed no further. Not that they were weary. How can twenty miles exhaust any ascending salmon? What is that distance compared with seventy river-miles in a day and an average of more than forty in a continuous gradient of fifteen hundred miles against the current?

As the water fell in, so progress slackened. Somehow the Two knew that no longer was there running-water above them. (I, standing on the bank, could see that the river had shrunk to thinly connected rungs in the ladder, which those fish in their watery home had sensed they could not climb.) They did a little prospecting in the reach above, but finding it bad ground on which to lie fell back. The water continued to fall in, which caused them to drop back still further.

In due course, after the next rise in water, they reached a wide pool formed by the junction of two forks of the river. Which way? Which way?

They lay in that pool and wandered round it, trying every turbulence they encountered. They made no attempt to move up, but awaited the next gentle spate. At last this came and brought an answer and also fair running-water in that stream which the answer had helped them to choose. It was a subtle message they received, something which either nostrils or receptors in the gills alone could interpret, a message (so man believes) which awakened a memory of their natal tributary.

Onwards and upwards. As they ascended, the banks came closer

Fair running-water

together and the speed of the current increased. In spite of the softer water of the mountain-bogs, they found, wherever it was broken, abundance of oxygen. Here and there, great granite boulders standing in the fairway divided the stream. They swam over stretches of sharp gravel; but those they passed by.

Early gales in September had stripped many leaves off the trees, especially those of sycamore and ash. These came floating passively down or scurried up and across stream before the wind. They spoke of mists shrouding a drear landscape and of the rapid waning of the year.

So many months without food, the constant call on reserves in making the ascent, the steady growth of the eggs, had taken toll of the Two. Their fine shape had disappeared. Bodies once brilliant silver and mauve had become greyish and dirty olive.

A company of fast-running salmon joined them in the pool in which they were lying, a pool shrunken owing to a spell of dry weather. Such is the attraction of any shoal for stray fish, that thereafter they all travelled up together. Possibly, the Two noticed the reddening ripeness of the males and the well-developed kype, the upturned hook of the lower jaw. But there was no semblance of any pairing, even though, as an angling writer of the eighteenth century remarked about lures, 'a scarlet coat is a maycrill bait for the ladies'.

In spite of the drain on their stored energy, the Two went thrusting their way, on and on, through rough water and smooth, until they entered a deep shelving pool below a spawning-ford. There they and the others of their company lay and waited.

Occasionally, one or two of the females went up to the gravel above, swam round and then dropped back, apparently satisfied with the reconnaissance. This, they must have realized, was indeed the Unknown Place to which they had so persistently struggled.

Hunter's Moon

Already it was the season of short days, when the nights drew out, colder and more dank. The Harvest Moon had been supplanted by the Hunter's Moon. The month of November was at hand.

One moonlight night a pair of itinerant otters on their way over the watershed came through the pool. Very easily they caught two of the salmon, which had relaxed their vigilance as fishes do, especially the Carps, just before and during the days of spawning. Perhaps the salmon were preoccupied with the uncomfortable pressure of swiftly ripening eggs and milt?

The other fish were frightened for the first time since they returned to the river. Otter-cubs had many weeks earlier fallen into the water nearby, as they shot down their slide. A great dog-otter had wandered along the edge of the water in search of his favourite freshwater mussels. But this savage invasion just below the redds was quite another matter. Seal! said their reflexes. That was enough.

At the very end of November there came a keen, frosty morning when she with the white patch moved up to the gravel-reach. Alone she went on her search for a small area suited to her needs. She found a place, where the stream trotted briskly down above her, and began her heavy labours according to the inherited plan.

She turned on her side, arched her body upwards and with tail and tail-fin made a series of rapid strokes, down and up. She thrashed the water into a strong turbulence, dislodging the stones and by the upward strokes sucking them into the current, so that it was able to carry them a short distance below and the fine material still further. This powerful fanning propelled her forwards, but she kept on returning to the original position.

Half a dozen strokes or so and she rested for five minutes. Yet the suction was strong enough to displace stones as big as nutmegs, as plover's eggs, as double walnuts, as duck's eggs.

The heap at the tail of the redd grew continually; and the pit over which she was working was always deepening. From time to time, she dropped into it and tested the depth with her extended anal fin.

A large, ugly-looking male in his reds and yellows had on the second day come up and had remained hovering below her. He had a proprietary air about him, but was content with watching the water go by. No redd-making for him. (How strange I thought that she should do all the work of constructing the pits and covering the eggs and yet have a better chance than he of regaining the sea!) Immediately, however, he saw her in the pit, he joined her and lay at her side, quivering in anticipation. But the moment had not arrived.

This was the first overture I had seen him make to her; although it may be that they had some understanding when in the pool below. (No-one has ever discovered when pairing takes place or which sex makes the first approach.)

From the instant when the male realized that the spawning-pit was almost ready, the association began; and it lasted as long as the Great Purpose was being pursued and was still unfulfilled.

Thenceforwards he mounted guard, chasing away all interlopers, especially ripe salmon-parr. And for her part, she would not tolerate the presence of any of her own sex, who tried to oust her from the redd. On the other hand, had she found her partner unequal to the task, she would not have hesitated to take on another—nor (and this is more likely) would he. But then he would have to fight pretty frequently with late-comers for his place on the new redd.

At length, she was satisfied with the depth of ten inches, to which the pit had been carried. She moved right down into it and, with tail raised and mouth open, let go the first batch of ripe eggs. They sank at once and were brought round by the back-eddy upstream toward the upper end of the pit, where they found safe niches.

An instant afterwards her partner, who was poised on an even keel, alongside and some inches below her, became highly excited and let go some milt. This followed the course taken by the eggs and flowed over them. Part of the Great Purpose had been consummated.

Then he moved away and did not return until the next pit was well advanced. Soon after that another batch of eggs was laid and he fertilized them.

One flower bribes with nectar bee or moth to carry abroad its pollen. Another scatters the tiny grains as dust before the wind. All quite impersonal. Clearly, this, too, was purely a business arrangement. Salmon-eggs are fertilized by favour of the current, which brings the gametes together, and with a very high degree of sureness. Affection? Love? Not a sign of it! A bucket in which to mix eggs and sperm serves equally well to achieve fertilization. Yet nothing, save the discipline enforced by free nature, can efficiently train, adjust and prune the young stock for the rigours of life in the river.

She with the white patch on her head stayed on. Once in possession of the redd, she did not let go until she had completed fully her part of the task. The male returned as often as a new batch of eggs had to be fertilized. Then again she went up a yard or two at a time and began working the gravel to form the next pit. With surprising quickness all her eggs were safely hidden by a deep layer of the larger size of material transported downstream by the current.

Like all her kind she put the eggs down deep; otherwise they would not have survived the attacks of the small, ever-hungry animals in the top layers of the redd. Neither could frost, nor any flood, save the abnormal, nor drought harm them. There was no intelligent design in her action, nor in the displacing of the stones, so freeing them of silt and fine sand, which is a great danger to buried eggs and an even greater danger to the young alevins during their early weeks.

31

She seemed to show no parental care; yet after she had shed her five thousand eggs into a series of pits, she still remained for a week on the redd, as though guarding it, and even though she never turned up anew any gravel she had previously sown.

In the end she who bore the white patch, already a fully-spent kelt, sank slowly back into quiet water and began her long journey back to the sea.

She who had been her companion of bright summer days was utterly exhausted. She lingered on the redds beyond her strength and, unable to withstand the relentless pressure and insidious sapping of flowing water, surrendered at last, as also did most of the male kelts, to the agent of that Prime Force which all of them had so long resisted.

So, also, do the leaves of the trees, the birds of the air and the sons of men.

> *Two tired salmon,*
> *All their labours done,*
> *Faced a tireless current.*
> *And then there was one.*

SPAWNING PAIR

Katabasis

WHEN THE FERTILE EGGS HAD BEEN LAID, THE ENDS of the circle met. A thought had been completed. Whatever might happen thenceforwards to the kelts or to those of them which recover and come in again for a second spawning, it has never been shown that they have any importance to the species. Their history lies outside the essential scheme, in which only maidens count. That the progeny of salmon returning for a second or third time has some influence upon the quality of the stock is an idea entirely lacking evidence. To find examples of Pacific salmon returning for a second spawning is rare and in some species quite unknown. Yet all the species survive and, but for man's interference, would prosper.

Now, in that river, which in imagination we see flowing at our feet, it is usual to find a good number of female kelts and a few males managing to recover fully enough to go out again to sea. The actual time taken in the descent of that or any other river is very uncertain. It is governed by the length of the downstream journey, by the character of the water traversed and, mainly perhaps, by the level at which the river runs at that period.

High spate is a condition kelts do not willingly face, until they are strong enough to control their own position. Inability to keep head to current must account for many casualties. They will, rather, take refuge from the press of water in quiet corners and await more favourable conditions.

I have often met those spent fish, when they had already descended far down the river. They had discarded their spawning-dress and were covered with a metallic sheen like that of lead freshly cut. Well-mended kelts they are usually then called; but it is rare to find any of them markedly improved in condition. It is rarer still to find a

35

Fresh-run springers

salmon-kelt that has been feeding on its way down, as do some sea-trout kelts. Yet every one of us has on some occasion been deceived into judging a hard-fighting, well-mended kelt to be a fresh fish. And, certainly, at the opening of the season they will take fly or minnow with embarrassing readiness.

Thus the kelts work their way down to the lower reaches and pass the fresh-run springers in their silver and mauve, eagerly ascending. Passing them without speaking to them, we are pretty sure, without giving them news from the upper waters. But often they pass on some of the maggots living in their gills, strange crustaceans which accompany sea-going adults and come back again, if their hosts do. Although all waters are alike to them, in fresh water alone can they breed.

This exchange of hosts within fresh water or a lucky invasion of resting fish by the larvae ensures the continuance of this race of parasites, the value of which to life has yet to be discovered.

In the spring following that spawning it happened that by the merest, but most happy chance, I was fishing the lowest beat of the river. At the first cast on the opening day my fly was taken almost fiercely, as it travelled across a quietly-flowing pool and hung close to the bank.

Ten minutes later I bent down and lifted out by the tail a kelt, a female kelt. In utter astonishment I looked at it. A most improbable thing had occurred. It was she with the white patch on her head. Not for an instant did I doubt it. No longer was she the dark emaciated slat of December. She shone with a typical false brilliance, which at first impression made her appear well nourished. As I lifted her on to the bank, to remove very tenderly the hook, her hollow flanks and shallow belly fell in. Length without depth!

My companion, whose business it is, marked her with one of his blue and yellow cylinders, gave her a number and set her free.

37

Wonderfully strong she was, too, for all her hazardous experiences. With great deliberation and on an even keel she moved into deep water. *Ave atque Vale!* I understood then something of what they felt, those who in early Colonial days bade farewell and waved to emigrants they were unlikely ever to see again, who sometimes through their tears watched their friends disappear, as the great sails filled to a favourable wind.

Of her with the white patch I never had news again.

One whose job it is to know something of salmon and their migrations remarked to me when I told him of that spring-time meeting that, a kelt having once reached salt water, the odds were certainly ten to one against its return as a clean fish. I think he may well be right.

She and other strong kelts will pass through the region that to us mean the sad plaint of the oyster-catcher and the flash of wheeling flocks of sandpipers, where replete cormorants sit lonely on long-forgotten posts far down the estuary and the surface of tidal water and swatchway is whipped up by the springtime gales. Out beyond the horizon she will go, where the grey curtains of rain traverse the sea.

It may be that her luck will hold on the passage outwards and that no coast-hunting otter, seal, porpoise, ray, shark or grampus will intercept her. So she will visit again the great feeding-areas, there to recover the weight and condition lost in accomplishing the cycle of life and then, perhaps, to add a little to the weight at which as a maiden she entered fresh water.

Six to eighteen months later the same risks must be run again on the inward journey. In between there are the customary sea-risks. That any, that five out of every hundred kelts that have regained the sea—which is the computed Irish rate—should return is remarkable.

It is so full of mystery this inexhaustible store in the great spaces of ocean, a mystery which must have seized the imagination of Matthew Arnold, when he wrote

Sand-strewn caverns, cool and deep,
Where the winds are all asleep;
Where the spent lights quiver and gleam;
Where the salt weed sways in the stream;
Where the sea-beasts rang'd all round
Feed in the ooze of their pasture-ground;
Where the sea-snakes coil and twine,
Dry their mail and bask in the brine;
Where great whales come sailing by,
Sail and sail, with unshut eye,
Round the world for ever and aye.

Life begins anew

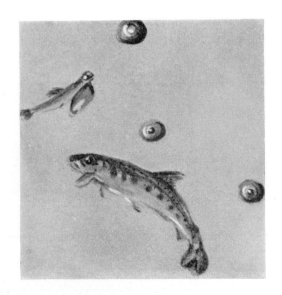

THE WORLD IN WHICH FISHES LIVE IS LARGELY
hidden from our eyes. Even in low and clear waters little enough
has been learnt of the way life goes on there. After all, the chances
of observing are few and unconnected. Something more has, however, been discovered by recent research.

I was thus given confidence that day, as I walked beside the
upland spawning-area, to peer through the mists of the future and
to divine part, at least, of the river-story of those salmon, which in
the fulness of time would issue forth from the eggs the Two had laid:
how those eggs had already started a new life-cycle: how only an
unbroken run of luck would enable a few of them to complete it.
And much else besides.

That which follows I discerned with the eye of prophecy. Only
for a brief period had the eggs been exposed to the outer world. They
sank at once to the bed of the pit, were carried a little up river and
found sanctuary amongst the gravel. Shortly afterwards they were

hidden by gravel displaced above them. This time they were hidden, not within the darkness of the salmon's body, but within that of the redd, eight, ten, twelve inches or even more. There during incubation cold, clear water will bathe them, its temperature at such times never differing to any marked degree from that of the cavity whence they had come.

When the eggs sank, they were already quick and were charged with fate. A few might fall by the way early, but many would perish later on. Some might be unable within the redd to resist the deadly fungus or avoid being choked, either as eggs or as alevins, should mud or silt force an entry. Some when they had become alevins would be assailed by the small invertebrates of the river, by rapacious fishes or by hunting birds. Some would survive to embark on their travels in the sea. A few would make their way back, in spite of all the perils

of sea and estuary, to yield profit to the netsman or to give sport to the angler. Fewer still would escape every hazard and ascend to the spawning-beds to complete their life-cycle, that another might begin.

Although one may reasonably assume that, at most, ten out of every four hundred eggs will perish in the redd, although only one out of that four hundred will finish the course, no-one knows which of them is so destined. The river-years hold a series of crises for the young fish; but how the impact of attrition falls and how the loss is distributed is entirely unknown. Predation is delivered at such

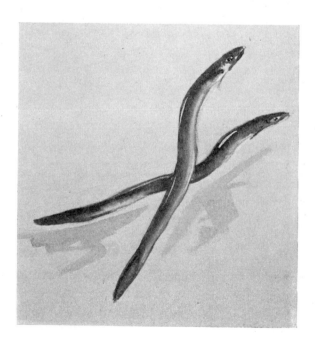

short range, that it can hardly be selective. In a hail of bullets the weakest may survive, the strongest may perish.

In the redds, at least, the eggs will be safely buried from the small animals that would prey on them, if they could intercept them. Thereafter the eggs with the principle of life within them will start along the road leading to the adult salmon in all its splendour and brilliance, in all its gracefulness and strength.

By the middle of December, if this mild weather last, thought I, looking down at the deserted redd, the eyes of these little fish will soon take shape as two small dark patches, visible in a rather blurred way through the translucent egg-shells and bearing witness to the life within. The eyes, the essential go-betweens, gathering and send-ing on messages by day and even by night from the outside world below the surface and above it: news of opportunities to be seized and warnings to be obeyed.

If there be no change in the weather, there will in the middle of January emerge from the eggs into the narrow corridors, deep within the gravel, a host of tiny Alevins, as they are called. They will be naked to the world, for the building of their scale-covering will not begin for some weeks. Nor until a few days have elapsed will their mouths be fully developed. As long as they continue, however, to draw nourishment from the store of food in the minute sac attached to the belly, all will be well.

Nearly seven weeks afterwards, about three months since those strenuous days their parents spent on the redd, they will creep up-wards to the surface of the gravel. There they will obtain their first glimpse of the light and of the world of water in which they will spend their lives.

All too early in the year! Hatching into a hard winter with its rigours, which create food-scarcity, often brings disaster to many

Upland spawning area

alevins, which are surely doomed as is a clutch of partridge-eggs at Christmastide. If only the river would run colder and so hold back growth within the egg! Such would postpone the day when those young alevins leave the gravel; and there will be ample food for the taking.

After the entry of the alevins into a free-swimming life, the store of food in the sac will be gradually reduced until it is exhausted. Very soon, however, after issuing from the redd, they will be forced, in order to obtain what they need for growth, to supplement the yolk, by hunting minute crustaceans and other small animals. When the sac is wholly absorbed, the young fish, which we then term Fry, will have to depend for their food entirely upon their skill at hunting.

The more expert they become in following and seizing their prey and the wider they range into the open, the greater the risks they will run from those larger animals, which, in turn, feed upon them: fierce carnivorous beetles and their larvae, nymphs of dragon-flies, alder-fly larvae and other rapacious creatures. Of this activity the jolly dipper is unquestionably innocent. The part played by the eel, if it be abroad in those early days, would be hard to assess.

Thus there sets in a period of predation that bears heavily, though healthily, on the stock. It will begin as soon as the alevins leave the redd and continue until the young fish have passed well out to sea as smolts.

A female salmon of average weight—twelve pounds or so—lays

about six thousand eggs. These represent a pair of fish. How insignificant by marine standards! And of every hundred eggs generally ninety reach the fry-stage. No wonder the young stock has to be so drastically reduced!

If, on the other hand, the population of a river, as a whole, were protected or permitted to survive, what a weak population would result! This thinning-out of numbers in fresh water means fewer mouths to fill and larger shares for all those which survive. That statement will serve; but actually the process is not quite as simple as that.

Soon vertical bars of sepia, the finger-marks, will have made their appearance on the flanks of the fry, which means that they will have entered the Parr-stage. This will take place two or three months after the absorption of the food-sac. All that period minute plates, the centres of the future scales, will have been forming, but very slowly. About six months and, perhaps, more will have to elapse, before those parr will be fully provided with a coat of scales. And the familiar red spots will be seen on and above the lateral line, when the young parr are an inch and a half long.

Thus feeding and growing, being eaten or by their agility avoiding that fate, those parr will pass through the summer's abundance and enter their first winter.

Throughout that part of the year there will always be available larval forms, especially stone-fly nymphs. But food is not then as great a problem as might appear. As the water grows colder, the parr will need less food, because digestion will be slowed down. And they will tend to keep mainly to their winter-quarters behind boulders, feeding but little and at times not at all, until favourable times return with the warmer water and the beginnings of abundance.

Thus there will come for those of this brood which have survived

WHERE MOTIONLESS HERONS STAND

up till then a second season of busy hunting. They will find insects, winged and immature, shrimps, snails and many small animals in weed-beds and amongst the stones. On such they will feed ravenously until high summer, when generally the water is too warm for that activity and there is a short check.

Although growth is in a sense fairly rapid, the weights attained are so small, so insignificant, compared with those accruing from two years of sea-feeding. Yet the length those parr will have reached by the opening of the year will, it seems, decide whether or not they shall migrate that year or the next. In the river we are now discussing it happens that parr spend either two years or three years in the fresh before venturing out to sea. The scales of those adults which had in the past returned to the river had told me that. But what a profound mystery it all is!

By the second winter the parr will be about four and a half to five inches long. I wondered whether by that autumn any of the males would be so strongly developed that they would be on the redds at spawning-time. I was thinking of one I had seen in attendance there the previous December, a most persistent opportunist. Fertilize the eggs that precocious parr could, notwithstanding his youth and inexperience, and may well have done. Even before the first batch of eggs was laid, his excited behaviour suggested that the female salmon was emitting something impalpable to our senses, which was being borne by the water and capable of attracting from afar, as does the taint of a vixen at clicketting-time. Or it may be his eyes were telling him what was about to happen.

The days of short commons—or is it, a disinclination to feed—will soon pass with the entry of the succeeding February. Some of those parr will then take advantage of the food available and add a little to their length, before they migrate. Others will not, but will go to sea just the same.

By the month of April the urge to drop steadily downstream will be upon them. That way leads to the sea, the Region of Measureless Abundance. If those young fish or any others have foreknowledge of the food to be obtained there, we do not in the least understand how it comes about.

Now, during the years of residence in the river, heavy toll will have been taken of the brood, especially so in the early months of life, when attack will have come from every quarter and every shortage of food will have been more keenly felt. Of those ninety fry about ten will remain to represent them as fully-grown parr, which will be about to turn into sea-going Smolts. As alevins and as small fry they will have been taken by trout, by loggerheaded chub and by other predators. The eel will have preyed on them in all stages, perhaps secretly by night. Pike and, now and then, herons will have caught them unawares. No-one knows how this loss is distributed; but more is yet to come, after the Great Departure has taken place.

The journey downstream, a long one for any of those parr which have remained in the upper reaches, will be accomplished slowly. Sometimes as much as four miles will be covered in a day, but generally it will be less. During the descent they are sure to meet other parr and will then proceed in company. The finger-markings on the flanks will be gradually obscured by the particles of the silver coat, which will then spread all over the scales. It will not, of course, replace them, for the original scales are borne throughout life, the

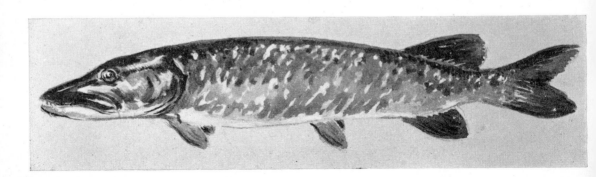

area of every one being added to, as the body of the fish increases its own area. Commonly the coat itself will be complete by the time the last pool above the tide, the Pool of Assembly, has been reached.

One day the pool will be full of smolts. The next morning all will have gone. Out by the sea-pool or down through the estuary, where motionless herons stand—sometimes in company—as sentinels guarding the runnels through which the ebbing tide flows, cutting deeply into the sand, so that the sides of the channels fall inwards.

The journey downstream

And straight out to sea they go. They do not linger around the estuary and in coastal waters in the region of sand-eel and inshore crustaceans, as do most seatrout smolts. They pass by this plentiful supply and, feeding as they travel, press toward the unknown.

Can these little migrants have any knowledge whither they are bound? It is hard, indeed, to avoid the answer. No. It is, however, in ill accord with the scheme of things that they should find the feeding-areas, which we presume all the survivors do, merely by chance.

In their bright new livery those smolts will run graver risks lower down, where salt water is undisputed master. Dogfish, the sea-angler's tope and coal-fish or saithe will be awaiting the young travellers. So will the hake, if it has by that time arrived from its winter home two thousand feet deep on the Atlantic Slope. And the

gannet, that feathered bomb, will join in the work, if it happens to be fishing near the river's mouth. Whether porpoise or seal thinks the smolt a morsel worth the trouble of catching nobody knows.

But those fortunate smolts of the brood which escape will go, as did their parents, out to the Region of Measureless Abundance, whence some of them will one day return, out to that Euphausia, that Somewhere which is to the east of the Great Abyss and south of the frigid sea-mountains and valleys descending from the Ultimate Isles.

DA CAPO.